On the Edg

Exciting Escapes

Jane Bingham

A+
Smart Apple Media

This book has been published in cooperation with Evans Publishing Group.

© Evans Brothers Limited 2011
This edition published under license from Evans Brothers Limited.

Published by Smart Apple Media
P.O. Box 3263, Mankato, Minnesota 56002

Produced for Evans Brothers Limited by
White-Thomson Publishing Ltd
Edited and designed by Paul Manning

Library of Congress Cataloging-in-Publication Data
Bingham, Jane.
  Exciting escapes / Jane Bingham.
     p. cm. -- (On the edge)
  Includes bibliographical references and index.
  Summary: "In a high-interest format, describes famous escapes from danger, including prison breaks, and escapes from kidnappers, wild animals, and natural disasters. Includes a quiz to test the likelihood of readers' ability to escape danger"--Provided by publisher.
  ISBN 978-1-59920-514-4 (library binding)
  1. Escapes--History--20th century--Juvenile literature. 2. Escapes--History--21st century--Juvenile literature. 3. Prisoner-of-war escapes--History--Juvenile literature. 4. Adventure and adventurers--History--Juvenile literature. 5. Prisoners--History--Juvenile literature. 6. Kidnapping--History--Juvenile literature. 7. Animal attacks--History--Juvenile literature. 8. Natural disasters--History--Juvenile literature. 9. Biography--20th century--Juvenile literature. 10. Biography--21st century--Juvenile literature. I. Title.
  G525.B54 2012
  904'.7--dc22
                              2010045446

Printed in the United States at Corporate Graphics in North Mankato, Minnesota.

Picture credits
Front cover, Getty/Mike Harrington; 3, 5, Photolibrary/Fotosearch; 6t, Shutterstock/K. West; 6b, © Bettmann/CORBIS; 7l, Alamy/Danita Delimont; 7r, Shutterstock/Kuznetsov Alexey; 8 (background), Shutterstock/Jonathan Noden-Wilkinson; 9, Jonathan F. Vance, Canada Research Chair, University of Western Ontario; 10b, Imperial War Museum; 11r, Imperial War Museum; 12, Edward Valachovic; 13, DPA/Picture-Alliance; 14t, Wikimedia Commons; 16t, Getty/John Lund; 17, Shutterstock/Mike Price; 18, Photolibrary/David McLain; 19, Shutterstock/John Kershner; 20, Image Source/Corbis; 22,Corbis/Whit Richardson; 23, ShutterstockVladimir Sazonov; 24, Photolibrary; 25, Getty Images; 26t, Corbis; 26b, Shutterstock/Clara; 27, Shutterstock/Frontpage.

The photograph of the Robertson family on page 16 was first published in *The Last Voyage of the Lucette* (Seafarer Books, 2005) and is reproduced by kind permission of Douglas Robertson.

5-2011
CAG1664

9 8 7 6 5 4 3 2 1

Contents

Devil's Island

For more than a hundred years, Devil's Island off the coast of French Guiana was one of the world's toughest prisons. The regime was brutal. Forgotten by the outside world, even the hardest men were reduced to despair—all except the prisoner they called Papillon.

🔺 Anyone planning to escape from Devil's Island faced terrifying risks. Massive waves swirled around the island's rocky shore. Man-eating sharks lurked in the ocean beyond.

THE MAN THEY CALLED PAPILLON

Nicknamed "Papillon" because of the butterfly tattoo on his chest,* Henri Charrière (1906–1973) was born in Ardèche, France, and became a well-known figure in the Paris underworld. Jailed for murder, he was sent to Devil's Island in 1931. After his final escape, he wrote a book about his life that became a worldwide bestseller. The book Papillon was also turned into a famous film with Steve McQueen and Dustin Hoffman.

*Papillon is French for butterfly.

Life on Devil's Island was a living hell. By day, the prisoners worked in water up to their waists, with the blazing sun beating down on their heads. At night, they sweated in their cells, attacked by snakes and giant spiders. The wardens told the men, "Put all hope out of your mind." But Papillon had a plan.

Watching Coconuts

Papillon had spotted a high, rocky cliff covered with coconut trees. He noticed how the coconuts fell into the sea and were carried past the jagged rocks. Gradually, he formed a daring escape plan, which he shared with his friend, Sylvain.

Leap to Freedom

In the dead of night, the two men climbed to the top of the cliff, carrying sacks filled with coconuts. Then they hurled themselves into the raging waves. They should have been smashed against the cliffs, but, miraculously, Papillon's plan worked. The sacks acted as rafts, and the men were carried out to sea. Sylvain drowned before they reached dry land, but after many more adventures, Papillon finally made it to freedom.

▼ *Once on the mainland, Papillon's ordeal was still not over. Ahead lay days of travel through thick jungle and crocodile-infested swamps.*

◄ *Prisoners who tried to escape from Devil's Island were kept for years in solitary confinement in tiny cells like this. Many died or went mad. Papillon survived.*

The Great Escape

During World War II, Stalag Luft III, the prison camp for captured Allied airmen in eastern Germany, was a name to inspire fear and dread. The Nazis claimed no one could escape from Stalag Luft—but they were in for a surprise.

In the spring of 1943, British airman Roger Bushell *(right)* held a top-secret meeting with fellow inmates at Stalag Luft III. Bushell had an ambitious plan. He proposed that three escape tunnels, code-named Tom, Dick, and Harry, would be dug, but only one would be chosen as the final escape route out of the camp.

◀ Each tunnel had to be dug 100 feet (30 m) below ground to conceal the sound of digging from the German guards. To prevent roof collapse, the walls were lined with wood scavenged from around the camp.

Over the next 10 months, 600 prisoners spent every spare minute digging the tunnels, secretly scattering the earth around the camp. By the following March, it was decided: tunnel Harry would be their escape route.

Into the Tunnel

At 10 p.m. on a freezing, moonless night, the Great Escape began. But the first man to emerge from the tunnel was in for a shock. He was still inside the perimeter fence! He ran swiftly for cover under a clump of trees. Then he waited silently as dozens of companions dashed to join him.

The Game's Up

At 4:55 a.m., prison guards spotted a man emerging from the ground. The game was up. As the guards searched the camp, 76 escapees climbed the prison fence and made a dash for it. Within days, 73 had been captured, but three escaped and eventually made it back to England. In a brutal reprisal ordered by Hitler, 50 of the unsuccessful escapees were shot.

After the escape, guards searched the camp to see what had gone missing. They found that the tunnelers had used 1,219 knives, 478 spoons, and 582 forks. Other missing items included 635 mattresses, 62 tables, 34 chairs, and 76 benches.

⬥ Two of the three successful escapees, Peter Bergsland (left) and Jens Müller (right). In the center is Norwegian Halldor Espelid, who was later caught and executed.

DIGGING THROUGH SAND

Stalag Luft was deliberately sited by the Germans in an area where the subsoil was yellow sand. This, they believed, would make tunneling nearly impossible. Also, it would be easy for the guards to spot signs of digging if they saw traces of yellow sand anywhere above ground.

Mission Impossible

Colditz fortress in eastern Germany looks like a castle in a horror movie. During World War II, it was where the Nazis sent their most dangerous prisoners of war. Almost all were hardened escapees, and all were determined to break out of Colditz—whatever the cost.

▼ Set on a hill overlooking the town, Colditz Castle's high walls made it a natural choice for a wartime prison.

One prisoner earned the title of "the greatest escapee of them all." Mike Sinclair *(right)* was a lieutenant in the British army. He was known as "the Red Fox" because of his red hair and his incredible cunning. In the space of just two years, Sinclair made three courageous attempts to escape from Colditz.

Sinclair's most cunning plan involved disguising himself as a prison guard. Meanwhile, two of his friends dressed as German sentries. Wearing his disguise, Sinclair ordered two real German sentries to swap places with his friends. The plan worked—until one of the Germans asked him for a password. Sinclair hesitated. The sentry raised the alarm. There was a scuffle and Sinclair was shot in the leg.

If at First You Don't Succeed...

For his second escape attempt, Sinclair and a friend climbed down a rope from a high window. Then they ran for their lives. They managed to reach the Dutch border before they were caught and sent back to Colditz.

Sinclair made his last bid for freedom alone. While he was exercising in a prison yard, he made a sudden dash for the fence, but only ran a few yards before he was shot dead. The man they called the Red Fox had made the ultimate sacrifice.

PLANE CRAZY!

One group of prisoners even planned to escape from Colditz by plane! Using stolen floorboards and electrical wire, they managed to build a glider and hide it in the roof of the prison chapel. Nobody knows if the glider would have worked. World War II ended before it could be launched.

◄ *Under the eyes of their German captors, Allied prisoners of war gather in the courtyard of Colditz Castle in 1943.*

Wall of Death

For almost 30 years, the German city of Berlin was divided by a massive wall. On the eastern side, a ruthless Communist regime controlled everyone's life. In West Berlin, people lived in freedom. The Wall was patrolled by guards with orders to shoot to kill. But this was not enough to stop some incredible escapes.

This area was known as the "death zone." Anyone entering it from the east would be shot on sight.

▼ Separating family and friends, the Berlin Wall was a hated symbol of the "Cold War" that divided Europe after World War II.

WALL FACTS

Erected: August 13, 1961
Dismantled: November 9, 1989
Total length: 87 miles (140 km)
Number of watchtowers: 302
Number of concrete bunkers: 20
Escapees killed: 192
Escapees shot/injured: app. 200

Graffiti and political slogans covered the Wall on the western side.

People tried many ways to escape from East Berlin. Some dug tunnels. Some hid in cars crossing the Wall at checkpoints. Perhaps the most daring escape of all was masterminded by two friends, Peter Strelzyk and Guenter Wetzel.

A Crazy Plan

In the spring of 1978, Peter and Guenter came up with a brilliant but risky plan. They started buying dozens of strips of lightweight cloth. Then they began to construct a giant hot-air balloon. After many false starts, they finally had a working balloon. But would it be strong enough to carry both families more than 15 miles (24 km) to freedom?

Into the Sky

Around 2 a.m. on September 16, 1979, the two men and their families climbed aboard the balloon. Then they lit the burner and rose into the sky, waiting anxiously for the wind to blow them in the right direction. After half an hour in the air, they began to run out of gas, and the balloon sank gently to earth.

In the darkness, it was hard to tell where they were at first. After hiding in a barn, they realized they had made it when they spotted a West German car. Their amazing escape made front-page news all around the world and inspired the 1981 Disney film *Night Crossing*.

The Wetzel family, photographed after their successful balloon escape to the West.

Breakout!

Alcatraz prison stands on a rocky island in San Francisco Bay in California. For 30 years it was home to America's most dangerous and hardened criminals. Prison wardens claimed that "the Rock" was completely escape-proof, but one man was determined to prove them wrong.

main cell block

parade ground

recreation yard

1.5 miles (2.4 km) to land

▶ *Separated from the mainland by treacherous currents, Alcatraz served as a federal prison from 1933 until 1963. Today, the island is a historic site operated by the U.S. National Park Service.*

Frank Lee Morris was no ordinary criminal. He was a highly intelligent man who had been masterminding crimes from the age of 13. As soon as he arrived at Alcatraz, he started planning his escape. He soon teamed up with three other prisoners: John and Clarence Anglin and Allen West.

If ever a man was destined for Alcatraz, it was Frank Lee Morris. A lawbreaker from his early teens, Morris spent years behind bars, serving sentences for every crime from narcotics possession to armed robbery.

Tunnels

Led by Morris, the men started digging tunnels into the main ventilation shaft—and preparing for a cold sea voyage. John Anglin glued more than 50 raincoats together to make a raft. Morris adapted an accordion to use as an air pump.

Dummy Heads

For the breakout to succeed, Morris and his friends needed to make the wardens believe that they were asleep in their cells as usual. They made dummy heads, using soap, toilet paper, and paint, plus some real hair from the prison barber. Before they escaped, they left the heads on their pillows. The dummies were simple, but they did the trick.

Dash for Freedom

On the night of June 11, 1962, Morris and the Anglin brothers crawled through a ventilation shaft and out onto the prison roof. (West was left behind because he hadn't finished digging his tunnel in time.) Then they climbed down 50 feet (15 m) of pipe and made a dash for the ocean. The three men were never seen again. Some claim they drowned at sea. Others believe they made it to freedom.

THE GHOSTS OF ALCATRAZ

Over the years, many inmates died in Alcatraz, and some believe their ghosts still haunt the island. Many former guards reported seeing ghostly apparitions while guarding the building, and visitors claim to have heard men screaming, whistling, and talking, and doors mysteriously clanging shut in the prison.

Hell in the Pacific

An experienced sailor, Dougal Robertson reckoned he was well-prepared for an around-the-world voyage. But when three killer whales capsized his yacht in the mid-Pacific, Dougal and his family found themselves pitched into a life-or-death struggle for survival on the high seas.

On January 27, 1971, Lyn and Dougal Robertson and their children set sail from England. They were looking forward to the trip of a lifetime. After a stormy start, the early part of their voyage went well. It was not until their yacht was 50 miles (80 km) off the Galapagos Islands in the Pacific Ocean that disaster struck.

△ *The Robertson family and their traveling companion Robin Williams in the tiny dinghy they were to share during their 37-day ordeal at sea.*

The whales hit the yacht with a deafening crash, knocking everyone off their feet. Within a few minutes, the boat was sinking. Adults and children thrashed around in the waves, praying that the whales would spare them.

Onto the Raft

By a miracle, everybody made it into the dinghy and the life raft being towed behind. But their problems had just begun. The tiny boats could barely carry six people. Food and water were in short supply. Nobody knew where they were, and there were sharks circling in the water all around them.

Dougal made a brave decision. Instead of heading south for land, he steered north into the Pacific Ocean. He knew that if the raft hit rocks, all his family would die.

◆ Killer whales are the largest members of the dolphin family. Despite their name, they are rarely a threat to humans.

Desperate

After 17 days, the raft began to sink and the Robertsons made their final, desperate move. Weak with hunger and exhaustion, they all transferred to their tiny dinghy and paddled slowly northward. On the 37th day, they were spotted and rescued by Japanese fishermen.

TURTLE BLOOD SOUP

On the life raft, the Robertsons survived by drinking turtle blood and catching fish with a spear made out of a paddle. Their tiny craft was so overladen that they were often up to their waists in water and had to take turns to sit on the only dry seat in the boat.

Tomb of Ice

In 1985, British mountaineers Joe Simpson and Simon Yates set out to scale the Siula Grande peak in the Andes Mountains. At 21,000 feet (6,400 m), it was a challenge. But they were experienced climbers. What could go wrong?

The first two days of the climb brought their share of narrow escapes. But when Simpson fell and broke his leg during the descent, things started to go seriously wrong.

Determined not to leave his companion to die on the mountain, Yates came up with a plan. Knotting two ropes together, he would lower his injured friend as far as the rope would allow, then climb down after him— and so on down the slope.

A climber uses an ice ax to scale the sides of a narrow crevasse.

Amazingly, the plan worked—for a time. Then, while lowering Simpson down the icy slope, Yates felt the rope suddenly tighten. Hidden from view below him, Simpson had careered off the edge of the mountain and was dangling over a huge crevasse. Worse still, the extra weight on the rope meant Yates was being slowly dragged after him!

Yates was faced with an agonizing dilemma. Should he save himself and let Simpson die? After hanging on for over an hour, he made his choice. He pulled out his knife and cut the rope.

Into the Ice Cave

Simpson plummeted into the crevasse. The fall should have killed him, but luckily he landed on a ledge of ice. He knew he had to keep moving. Slowly and painfully, he pulled out his rope and started rappeling into the ice cave.

Unable to climb up, Simpson knew his only hope was to crawl further down in search of a way out. Every step was agony, but eventually he saw light from below. He was in luck!

Back from the Dead

Meanwhile, convinced that Simpson must be dead, Yates made his way slowly back to base camp. His decision to cut the rope had been the hardest he had ever faced—but what else could he have done?

He was preparing to leave when he heard faint, desperate cries for help. It was Simpson. Amazingly, after escaping from the ice cave, he had dragged himself down the mountain. Starving, dehydrated, and delirious, he was still alive!

WHAT WOULD YOU DO?

Vividly described in his book Touching the Void, Simpson's escape from Siula Grande is one of the great mountaineering stories of all time. Some climbers criticized Yates for cutting the rope to avoid being dragged over the edge of the precipice. Simpson always defended his friend's action. What do you think? What would YOU have done?

The spectacular peak of Siula Grande in the remote Peruvian Andes.

Shark Attack!

Wedge-shaped head makes it easy for shark to twist and turn

Electrical sensors in upper body detect muscle movement of prey

Teeth specially adapted to tear through flesh, bone, and turtleshell

In a contest between a fully grown tiger shark and an unsuspecting surfer, the smart money has to be on the shark. But 17-year-old Hoku Aki was quick-thinking—and he was determined not to go down without a fight.

▲ *With its powerful jaws and razor-sharp teeth, a tiger shark can devour anything and everything in its path. As well as the remains of human victims, the stomachs of dead tiger sharks have been found to contain gasoline cans, baseballs—even car tires.*

Brennecke Beach on the Hawaiian island of Kauai is a popular surfing spot. On the afternoon of September 25, 2002, Hoku Aki, a confident body-boarder, was standing about 150 feet (45 m) out to sea in murky water, waiting for the perfect wave. Suddenly, he saw a huge shadow moving through the water toward him. He felt a violent impact followed by an agonizing pain in his leg.

Pain and Shock

"I opened my eyes and saw the shark," he said. "It was tossing me all over the place. I heard my leg break. I heard the bone snap."

Hoku thought he was going to die. The ferocity of the attack was terrifying. But Hoku kept his nerve—and fought back.

Fighting Back

While the shark twisted and turned in the water, Hoku yelled and waved his arms. He tried to pry the shark's jaws open. When that didn't work, he made a grab for one of its eyes. "I grabbed the shark's eye and ripped it out, and he let me go."

In moments, Hoku was dragged to safety by shocked onlookers. A nurse rushed to give him first aid. By the time a lifeguard arrived on the scene, the bleeding had stopped. It wasn't until later that Hoku realized how lucky his escape had been. He had lost a foot, but raw courage and quick reflexes had almost certainly saved his life.

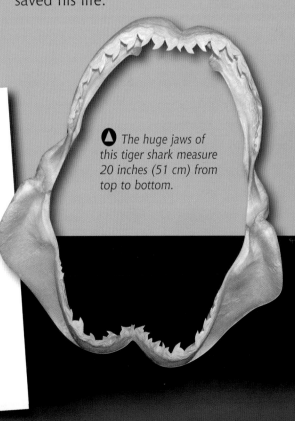

⬥ The huge jaws of this tiger shark measure 20 inches (51 cm) from top to bottom.

SHARK FACTS

- In 2000, the year with the most recorded shark attacks, 79 were reported worldwide, 16 of them fatal.
- Since 1852, the United States has had the most shark attacks (1,032) followed by Australia and South Africa.
- The location with the most recorded shark attacks is New Smyrna Beach, Florida.
- It is estimated that a person's chance of getting attacked by a shark is one in 11.5 million.

Life or Limb?

Trapped without hope of rescue in a remote
corner of the Utah desert, climber and
"canyoneer" Aron Ralston faced the
most agonizing decision of his life.
Be warned: The harrowing story
of his escape from Blue
John Canyon is not for
the squeamish . . .

On April 26, 2003, 28-year-old Aron Ralston set out on foot for Blue John Canyon in the Utah desert. An experienced canyoneer, Aron loved the outdoor life and was looking forward to a good day's climbing.

He was inching his way down a narrow part of the canyon when he heard a roar. High above him, a massive boulder had come loose. He tried to snatch his arm away, but it was too late. As the rock fell, his hand was crushed beneath it, pinning him to the canyon wall.

A Living Nightmare

In agonizing pain, Aron tried everything. He chipped at the rock with his knife. He used a rope to try to hoist the boulder off his hand. When that failed, he started thinking hard. Nobody knew where he was. And his food and water would run out in a couple of days.

⮟ Canyoneering is the sport of exploring canyons using a range of climbing and athletic skills. Here, a canyoneer lowers himself down a waterfall in Zion National Park, Utah.

Decision Time

By day five, Aron knew there was only one way out. Using the boulder for leverage, he snapped the bones in his forearm. Next, he tied a strap tightly below his elbow to make a tourniquet. Then he braced himself for the terrible task of sawing through his own flesh with a blunt knife. After an hour of agony, he was free, but he still had to climb down the canyon and hike back to his truck. Somehow, Aron managed to cover 5 miles (8 km), before he met a family who summoned help.

Now fitted with an artifical arm, Aron still goes climbing alone—but never without telling his friends where he's going first!

A ROCK AND A HARD PLACE

In the book he wrote about his ordeal, Aron describes the moment he cut into his own flesh: "It was a hundred times worse than any pain I've felt before, but it was also the most beautiful thing I've ever felt. All the joys of a future life came rushing into me. Maybe this is how I handled the pain. I was so happy to be taking action."

Kidnapped!

Here's a challenge: Imagine being held up at gunpoint, bound and gagged, bundled into a pickup truck, and held captive in lonely woods far from home. Now try and escape —using only a safety pin!

On a quiet day in a suburb in Florida, 13-year-old Clay Moore was waiting for the school bus with his friends. Suddenly a pickup truck skidded to a halt, and an armed man jumped out. Pointing his gun at Clay, he ordered him into the truck. Clay's friends watched in horror as the door slammed shut and the truck raced off toward the woods.

△ Faced with an armed attacker, Clay Moore had to think fast. He knew his friends would sound the alarm. But in the meantime, how could he outwit his captor?

Inside the truck, Clay's mind was racing. He was determined to escape from his kidnapper. But how? Then he remembered the safety pin his mother had given him that morning to mend a tear in his school uniform. Taking care not to let his captor see, he removed it from his jacket and hid it in his mouth. Already a plan was taking shape in his mind.

Bound and Gagged

After half an hour, the truck came to a halt. Clay's wrists and ankles were bound with shoelaces and duct tape. A sock was stuffed in his mouth and his eyes and mouth were covered with more tape. Finally, the kidnapper stuck a bag over Clay's head and dumped him by a tree.

Breaking Free

Hearing the kidnapper leave the scene, Clay set to work. He shook the bag off his head and managed to spit out the sock and the safety pin. Using his bound hands, he rubbed the tape off his eyes. Then, picking up the safety pin in his teeth, he used it to loosen the laces around his ankles and wrists.

After a desperate hour, Clay struggled free. He scrambled through the woods and across fields until he spotted a farmer and used his phone to call home. Shortly after, he was joyfully reunited with his family.

◀ *Clay Moore with a local police officer at a press conference held following his dramatic escape.*

WHO KIDNAPPED CLAY?

Clay's kidnapping was a terrifying ordeal not only for him, but for his family. Fortunately, his friends were able to give police a full description of the kidnapper and his truck. Investigators traced the truck to a farm, where they also found a scribbled ransom note. An illegal migrant worker, Vicente Beltran-Moreno, 22, was later charged with the crime.

Jungle Miracle

When her plane fell out of the sky and plunged into the Amazon rain forest, Juliane Koepcke's chances of survival were practically nil. But miraculously, she managed to walk away from the crash—and to survive a grueling 10-day trek through the jungle.

▲ *Juliane Koepcke, photographed shortly after her miraculous escape from death in the Amazon rain forest.*

On Christmas Eve 1971, 17-year-old Juliane Koepcke, a German high school student living in Lima, Peru, was traveling with her mother in a small passenger plane flying east over the Amazon rain forest. Forty minutes into the flight, the plane hit a thunderstorm. Juliane saw a lightning flash and felt the plane lurch. "We were headed straight down. Christmas presents were flying around the cabin, and I could hear people screaming." Then she blacked out.

Still strapped in her seat, she woke to find herself falling through the air. With a terrible crash, she hit the trees. As she lay bruised and bleeding on the jungle floor, the horror of her situation began to dawn on her. Her collarbone was broken. She was hundreds of miles from civilization. Worst of all, she was alone.

▶ *The Amazon jungle where Juliane's plane came down is one of the most hostile environments on Earth.*

Rain Forest Journey

Juliane's survival up to this point was amazing enough, but the story of how she made it back to civilization through the Amazon rain forest is even more remarkable.

By the next morning, she knew beyond a doubt that she was the only survivor of the crash. Wielding a stick to ward off snakes and spiders, Juliane followed a stream for seven days before she spotted a small hut in a clearing in the jungle. Starving, delirious, and plagued by insect bites, she took shelter there for three days before being found and rescued by a group of local loggers.

◀ *Struck by lightning, Juliane's plane exploded in mid-air 10,000 feet (3,000 m) above the rain forest. Juliane fell to earth still strapped into her seat. She escaped the crash with just a broken collarbone.*

HOW DID SHE SURVIVE?

Juliane is one of a tiny handful of people to have survived a fall from an aircraft flying at such a great height. The daughter of a zoologist, Juliane had a good knowledge of the rain forest. She also remembered her father saying that following a stream always leads you back to civilization.

Escapee's Quiz

Could you tunnel your way out of a prisoner-of-war camp or lead an escape from the world's toughest prison? Check your score on the Escape-o-meter with this easy-to-answer quiz.

1   As a prisoner of war, your fellow prisoners in Stalag Luft ask you to help them dig an escape tunnel. Do you:
    a   Immediately report them to the guards?
    b   Refuse to get involved in case it all goes wrong?
    c   Roll up your sleeves and get digging?

2   While climbing in the Alps, you see an avalanche of snow racing toward you. Do you:
    a   Stand rooted to the spot and scream for help?
    b   Run as fast as you can in the opposite direction?
    c   Crouch low behind a rock and turn away from the avalanche, with your hands covering your nose and mouth?

3   While escaping from Colditz Castle disguised as a nun, you are stopped and challenged by one of the guards Do you:
    a   Shrug your shoulders and give yourself up?
    b   Pull a gun and open fire?
    c   Smile sweetly and pretend to be hard of hearing?

4   During a school trip abroad, your bus is hijacked by armed bandits and driven to a remote mountain hideout. Do you:
    a   Stay put and wait for help to arrive?
    b   Wait until nobody's looking and make a break for it on your own?
    c   Memorize the route and start thinking about organizing an escape attempt with your most trusted friends?

5   Panic breaks out when your underground train is stranded in the middle of a tunnel. Do you:
    a   Scream and fight your way to the nearest exit?
    b   Crouch in a corner and try to avoid getting hurt?
    c   Calm the other passengers down and try to lead them to safety?

CHECK YOUR SCORE

Mostly a Avoid escapes: Risky situations are not for you!

Mostly b You have a strong instinct for survival, but you don't always think things through.

Mostly c Congratulations—you have the makings of a successful escapee!

Glossary

apparition a visible ghostly presence

bunker concrete guard post or shelter

canyon deep valley between cliffs

canyoneer climber who explores canyons

captor someone who holds another person prisoner

checkpoint a border crossing point between two countries

code name secret name for something or someone

Cold War period of high tension between eastern and western Europe after World War II

collarbone bone joining breastbone to shoulder blades

Communism system of government where all property is shared

crevasse a deep open crack in a glacier or ice field

federal belonging to, or controlled by, central government

lieutenant an officer in the army or navy

Nazis German followers of Hitler during the 1930s and World War II

perimeter the edge or outer limits of an area

press conference meeting held to announce or publicize something

rappel to lower yourself down on a rope

recreation yard place where prisoners can exercise

regime rulers of a country or organization

reprisal act of punishment or revenge for something

ruthless showing no mercy or human feeling

scavenge to collect or gather from whatever happens to be lying around

sensor device or organ that detects, for example, heat or movement

sentry a soldier who keeps watch or guard

solitary confinement locking someone away on their own as a punishment

Stalag Luft short for "Stammlager Luft," or permanent camp for airmen

suburb residential area outside the city center

underworld network of criminals or organized crime

ventilation shaft tunnel or pipe allowing air to circulate

warden a prison guard

Web Sites and Further Reading

Web Sites

www.alcatrazhistory.com/mainpg.htm
Detailed information about the United States's most feared maximum-security prison and its inmates.

www.pbs.org/wgbh/nova/greatescape/
A site describing 10 great escapes in history.

www.historyonthenet.com/WW2/great_escape.htm
A site on the escape from Stalag Luft III during World War II, including activities and a quiz.

Further Reading

Breakouts and Blunders, John Townsend (Raintree, 2006)

Desperate Escapes, Simon Lewis, (Smart Apple Media, 2009)

Great Escapes, Charlotte Guillain (Heinemann, 2012)

Great Escapes, Ann Weil (Raintree, 2007)

Index